THE 12 BIGGEST BREAKTHROUGHS IN
FOOD TECHNOLOGY

by Marne Ventura

www.12StoryLibrary.com

12-Story Library is an imprint of Peterson Publishing Company and Press Room Editions.

Produced for 12-Story Library by Red Line Editorial

Photographs ©: Ppart/Shutterstock Images, cover, 1; Somchai Rakin/Shutterstock Images, 4; Paul Goldberg/AP Images, 5; Denis Vrublevski/Shutterstock Images, 6; Vicky Jirayu/ Shutterstock Images, 7; HandmadePictures/Shutterstock Images, 8; Rever/Shutterstock Images, 9; Sergej Razvodovskij/Shutterstock Images, 10; Hamik/Shutterstock Images, 11; Library of Congress, 12, 15; Yulia Davidovich/Shutterstock Images, 13; sspopov/ Shutterstock Images, 14, 29; Brian Mueller/Shutterstock Images, 16; Marjory Collins/Library of Congress, 17; Hemera Technologies/Thinkstock, 18; Louis Cukrov/Shutterstock Images, 19; Vladimir Kim/Shutterstock Images, 20; NASA/Rex Features/AP Images, 21; Itman47/ Shutterstock Images, 22; AP Images, 23; Adisa/Shutterstock Images, 24; Alexandra Lande/ Shutterstock Images, 25, 28; Fotokostic/Shutterstock Images, 26; Tiger Gallery/Shutterstock Images, 27

ISBN
978-1-63235-014-5 (hardcover)
978-1-63235-074-9 (paperback)
978-1-62143-055-1 (hosted ebook)

Library of Congress Control Number: 2014937353

Printed in the United States of America
Mankato, MN
June, 2014

Go beyond the book. Get free, up-to-date content on this topic at 12StoryLibrary.com.

TABLE OF CONTENTS

Cooking with Fire 4

Farming 6

Canning 8

Gas Stove 10

Breakfast Cereal 12

Pasteurization 14

Electric Refrigerator 16

Iodized Salt 18

Freeze-Drying 20

The Green Revolution 22

Flash-Freezing 24

Genetically Modified Organisms 26

Fact Sheet 28

Glossary 30

For More Information 31

Index 32

About the Author 32

EARLY PEOPLES LEARN TO COOK WITH FIRE

Scientists are not sure when early humans first cooked food. The best proof was found in a cave in Israel. Bits of bones were uncovered in the ashes there. Flint tools were found nearby. Burnt bones were discovered in other parts of the cave. Experts think people living there made fires and cooked meat approximately 300,000 years ago. Other sites have suggested that humans may have been using cooking fires as much as 1 million years ago.

Whenever it first happened, learning to use fire for cooking was a huge turning point for ancient humans. The heat kills harmful bacteria.

Fire provided the earliest cooking method.

6.5

Width in feet (2 m) of an ancient cooking hearth discovered in a cave in Israel.

- Fire was used approximately 300,000 years ago in modern-day Israel.
- Led to better health and social development.

FOOD SCIENCE

Food scientists search for new ways to help farmers and food producers to provide safe, healthful foods for all people. They study which foods are best to eat and how to keep foods fresh longer. They look for better ways to prepare food and how to transport food to people who need it.

Burnt bones and ash found in a cave in South Africa suggest that early humans may have made fires there.

This makes food safer to consume. Cooked foods are also easier to chew and digest. After they started cooking with fire, humans absorbed more nutrients from what they ate. This made their bodies, and especially their brains, work better. Cooking fires served another purpose, as well. They were a place where early peoples gathered and socialized.

EARLY AGRICULTURE CHANGES SOCIETY

For thousands of years, people had to hunt for their food. They gathered roots, fruit, seeds, and leaves. They made primitive weapons to hunt animals. They had to move constantly from place to place to find enough food. It was a hard, dangerous life.

Approximately 10,000 years ago, a group of people living near the Dead Sea started saving the seeds of wild wheat plants. They planted the seeds to grow more wheat.

Wheat was one of the first crops grown by early humans.

1,000

Approximate years after farmers started growing crops that they began raising animals for food.

- Agriculture began in approximately 8,000 BCE in the Middle East.
- Lessened need for hunting and gathering.
- Led to beginning of cities and civilization.

They could plant enough grain in the wet season to last through summer droughts. Historians believe they were the first farmers. The population expanded into other parts of the Middle East. These early farmers soon were growing wheat, barley, peas, and beans. Around the same time, people in the area of modern-day China started growing rice. And evidence has been found that squash was being grown in modern-day Mexico.

Farming changed the way people lived. They no longer had to travel to find food. They built homes and

Farmers have been growing rice in the area of modern-day China for thousands of years.

lived together in villages. Farmers grew enough food for many people. This freed others to do different kinds of work. Societies that were more complicated and varied soon developed.

CANNING KEEPS FOOD FRESH LONGER

Until the early 1800s, sailors had no way to keep food fresh on long trips. They ate mostly salted meat and dry bread. Many became sick from scurvy. This illness was caused by poor nutrition. Then the French navy decided to hold a contest. A cash prize would go to the person who came up with a new way to keep food fresh.

Chef Nicolas Appert had noticed that when he heated food in sealed glass jars, it didn't spoil as quickly. He entered the contest. The sailors tried taking jars of meat, fruit, vegetables, and milk to sea. The food stayed fresh longer. And fewer sailors were dying of poor nutrition.

Canning food can keep it fresh for years.

In 1810, English inventor Peter Durand improved on Appert's idea. He heated food in sealed tin cans instead of glass. The airtight seal kept bacteria from growing inside. Cans were better for sailors and explorers because they didn't break. At first, the process was expensive and time-consuming. And since there were no can openers, it took a hammer and chisel to open one.

In 1866, the can opener was invented. Soon new factories made cans of food more quickly. They used lighter-weight tin, which cost less. More people than ever had access to canned foods.

200 billion

Approximate number of cans of food produced worldwide each year.

- Canning was introduced in 1810 in France.
- First used to keep food fresh for sailors and travelers.
- Made healthful preserved foods available to more people.

The development of canning led to the invention of the can opener.

FOOD PRESERVATION

Before canning, foods were preserved by removing all the liquid. This stopped bacteria from growing. But the process was time-consuming, and dried foods had fewer nutrients. Another method, called curing, involved adding salt to stop bacteria growth.

4

USER-FRIENDLY GAS STOVES TAKE OFF

Once people learned to cook with fire, they built outdoor ovens of stone. They burned wood to produce the heat needed to bake bread or cook food in pots. Later, they cooked food in kettles hung over fireplaces inside the home. The fire kept the kitchen warm, but it made the walls sooty. Flying sparks could set a house on fire.

By the 1800s, many people used cast-iron stoves instead of fireplaces. These stoves used up to 50 pounds (23 kg) of wood or coal per day. It was easy to get burned when adding fuel. They also took up a lot of space.

By the end of the 1800s, companies were piping natural gas into homes to power lamps. As more people switched to electric lighting, inventors came up with another

10

Early gas stoves had to be lit with a match. Modern gas stoves light automatically, using a pilot light.

use for gas. Inventors designed stoves that used gas instead of wood or coal. A British inventor made a stove that was smaller than a wood- or coal-burning stove. The outside surface stayed cool. Because it used piped-in gas, the cook didn't need to add wood or clean out the ashes. Other companies began to make better gas stoves and ovens. By 1915, ovens had a dial that let the cook control the temperature.

Many people like gas stoves because the cooktop heats up and cools down quickly.

40

Percentage of US homes that now have gas stoves. Most other homes have electric stoves.

- Gas stoves were invented by James Sharp in 1826.
- Safer, cleaner, and more convenient than open fire.
- Have built-in temperature control.

MICROWAVE OVENS

In 1946, a researcher was working with a kind of electromagnetic wave called a microwave. When he got close to the machine producing the waves, he noticed that the candy bar in his pocket melted. He started exposing other foods to the waves to see what would happen. Corn kernels popped. An egg heated up and then exploded. The researcher realized that this technology could be used to heat and cook food. Today, most homes in the United States have a microwave oven in the kitchen.

BREAKFAST CEREALS REPLACE HIGH-FAT BREAKFASTS

Early humans used stones to grind wheat or barley. They added water and boiled the grains. Porridge, or boiled grain, was a staple for Roman soldiers. In the Middle Ages, people ate porridge made from oats. Early American settlers used corn. After the Industrial Revolution, many people had more money to spend on breakfast. They ate more meat and eggs to start the day.

Doctors started to learn that high-fat diets led to health problems. In the mid-1800s, Dr. James Caleb Jackson started serving a new kind of breakfast at a health spa. He made it by baking ground wheat mixed with water. It was so hard that it had to be soaked in milk overnight before being eaten. He started marketing the food as Granula.

MAKING SHAPES

Cereal makers started using molds to make different shapes of cereals. A mixture is poured into a barrel and then heated. Next it is pushed through a mold cut in a shape, such as an O. Different shapes of dies are used to make breakfast cereal, snack foods, and pasta.

John Kellogg, inventor of corn flakes, helped make breakfast cereals popular.

Now breakfast cereals come in many different textures, shapes, and flavors.

A doctor named John Kellogg noticed that people were buying Granula. He wanted to make a better breakfast food. He began to experiment. One day he left a batch of overcooked wheat grains to dry. The grains separated into flakes. This became the first flaked cereal. Soon companies were making corn flakes, wheat flakes, puffed rice, and toasted oats. It was the birth of breakfast cereal. It was one of the first foods to be marketed as a health food. Later use of processed grains and sugars made many cereals less healthful.

THINK ABOUT IT

Today, cereal makers print a nutrition label on the box. It includes information about the cereal's ingredients and nutrients. How do you think people should use this information?

40

Number of cereal brands that had sprung up by 1902 around Battle Creek, Michigan, a hotspot for the cereal industry.

- The first breakfast cereal was invented by James Caleb Jackson in 1863.
- Changed breakfast from a high-protein to high-fiber meal.
- Led to the breakfast cereal industry.

13

PASTEURIZATION MAKES FOOD SAFER

When most people lived in rural areas, they got fresh milk from cows on nearby farms each day. It didn't need to be kept cold because they drank it right away. In the 1800s, more people began to live in cities. Milk was brought from farms on horse-drawn wagons. It often spoiled during the long trip. People who drank the milk were getting sick.

Louis Pasteur was a French scientist. Pasteur discovered that bacteria in the air and soil caused milk and other foods to spoil. Some of these tiny organisms also caused

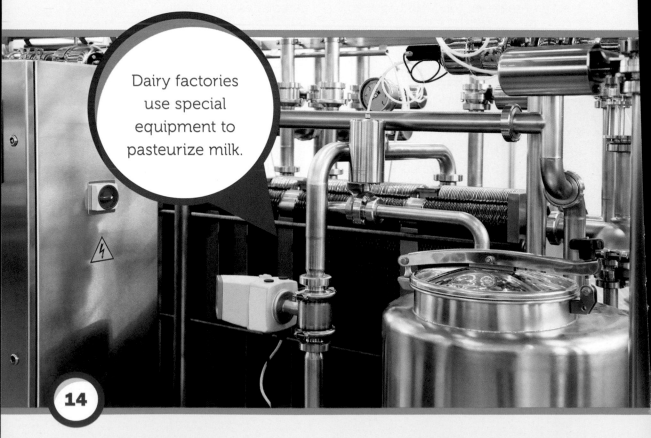

Dairy factories use special equipment to pasteurize milk.

160

Recommended temperature in degrees Fahrenheit (71°C) used to pasteurize apple juice.

- Discovered by Louis Pasteur in 1864.
- Heated milk to kill bacteria.
- Now used on milk and other food products.

EDIBLE FOOD WRAP

Scientists are finding new ways to kill harmful bacteria. New kinds of edible food wrap are being made from herbs, crab shells, and egg whites. These foods are chosen because they stop bacteria or mold growth. The wraps are invisible and tasteless. They can be used to wrap foods such as sandwiches. They keep food safe and cut down on waste.

diseases. He found that heating milk killed the bacteria. This process became known as pasteurization.

Farmers began to pasteurize milk in the 1920s. The process involves heating the milk to a temperature of 145 degrees Fahrenheit (63°C) for 30 minutes. It can also be heated to higher temperatures for shorter periods of time. This kills disease-causing bacteria such as salmonella and E. coli. Pasteurized milk can be stored longer. Juices and other foods can be pasteurized, as well.

French scientist Louis Pasteur figured out how to use heat to kill bacteria.

ELECTRIC REFRIGERATION REDUCES FOOD SPOILAGE

Thousands of years ago, people figured out that cold food stayed fresh longer. They stored food in caves and cool streams. Later, people dug underground cellars and filled them with snow and ice. But ice melted quickly in warm weather. Sometimes it wasn't available at all.

In the late 1800s, many Americans had an icebox in the kitchen. The iceboxes were made of wood and lined with tin. Blocks of ice made in factories were delivered to homes on wagons. Every day, a water tray had to be emptied. In the meantime, inventors were experimenting with other cooling methods. They found that certain chemicals absorbed heat when turned into vapor. This cooled down the inside of the refrigerator. Ammonia was used for a while, but it was toxic. Inventors continued to look for safer options.

In 1913, Fred Wolf introduced the first electric refrigerator for home use. It could be attached

Fred Wolf also invented ice cube trays.

Electric refrigerators were common in households by the 1940s.

1 million

Approximate number of electric refrigerators sold by General Electric in 1927.

- First home model introduced in 1913.
- Enabled people to store food longer.
- Let people eat safer, more nutritious food.

to an existing icebox. It was small and inexpensive. He called it the Domestic Electric Refrigerator, or Domelre for short. Soon, other companies were selling refrigerators. People could store and eat fresh foods with less effort and cost than ever before.

IODIZED SALT PREVENTS HEALTH PROBLEMS

In the early 1900s, as much as one-third of the population in parts of the United States had goiters.

A goiter is a bump on the neck. It can press against the windpipe and make it hard to breathe. A pregnant woman with a goiter might have a baby with birth defects or brain damage.

Two doctors in Ohio wanted to find a cure for this problem. They discovered that people get goiters when they do not get enough of the nutrient iodine. Iodine is an element found in seawater and some rocks and soil. The human body doesn't make iodine, but it needs it to stay healthy. The doctors started giving iodine supplements to patients. People taking the supplements did not get goiters.

Companies that sold table salt began to add iodine to the product. This helped more people add iodine

SELL BY ↑

TO OPEN

PUSH UP HERE

VITAMIN D MILK

TO OPEN

GRADE A PASTEURIZED HOMOGENIZED

Nutrition Facts
Serving Size 1 cup (240mL)
Servings Per Container 8

Amount Per Serving

Calories 150	Calories from Fat 70
	% Daily Value*
Total Fat 8g	12%
Saturated Fat 5g	25%
Cholesterol 35mg	11%
Sodium 130mg	5%
Total Carbohydrate 12g	4%
Dietary Fiber 0g	0%
Sugars 12g	
Protein 8g	

Vitamin A 8%	Vitamin C 2%
Calcium 30%	Iron 0%
Vitamin D 25%	

* Percent Daily Values are based on a 2,000 calorie diet. Your daily values may be higher or lower depending on your calorie needs:

INGREDIENTS: MILK WITH 400 IU VITAMIN D ADDED PER QUART.

VITAMIN D MILK

Many dairy products are fortified with vitamin D.

Great Tasti

18

Salt Savvy BY MORTON

TIPS ON BACK

MORTON SALT

THIS SALT DOES NOT SUPPLY IODIDE, A NECESSARY NU

MORTON® SALT HOUSEHOLD HINT #1

See copy on side panel

MORTON® IODIZED SALT

THIS SALT SUPPLIES IODIDE, A NECESSARY NUTRIENT.

NET WT. 26 OZ. (1 LB., 10 OZ.) 737 g

In 1924, Morton became the first company to start adding iodine to table salt.

70

Percentage of table salt sold in the United States that is iodized.

- Iodine was first used in 1924 as a treatment for goiters.
- Iodized salt prevents health problems.
- Led to other foods being fortified with vitamins and minerals.

to their diets. Soon, goiters and birth defects from lack of iodine became rare.

Like iodized salt, many foods are now fortified by adding nutrients. Flour loses most of its vitamins and minerals when it is processed. Millers enrich flour by adding nutrients back into the final product. Vitamins A and D are added to milk. Many breakfast cereals also have added vitamins and minerals. These foods help people take in the nutrients they need to stay healthy.

FREEZE-DRYING PRESERVES AND SHRINKS MEALS

In 1938, coffee farmers in Brazil had more coffee beans than they could sell. Scientists at Nestlé found a new way to keep the coffee fresh for a long time. The ground beans were frozen and placed in a vacuum. This removed the moisture. The coffee stayed fresh in a jar or pack.

Hot water was added later to make coffee drinks. Soon, food scientists tried this method of freezing and drying food to preserve other foods. Now, there are freeze-dried vegetables, herbs and spices, fruits, soups, and meals for campers.

Coffee was the first food product to be freeze-dried.

Astronauts have been using freeze-dried foods in space since the 1960s.

Freeze-drying foods also makes them lighter and smaller. Freeze-dried foods can be stored for long periods without refrigeration. This made them ideal for astronauts to take into space. Scientists made freeze-dried foods such as ice cream, shrimp, chicken and vegetables, butterscotch pudding, and applesauce. The food is stored in plastic bags or boxes. Astronauts add hot or cold water to make a meal. The first space foods were not very tasty. But as freeze-drying and packaging technology improved, so did the food.

98

Percentage of nutrition that is kept when a food is freeze-dried to 20 percent of its original weight.

- Freeze-drying was introduced in 1938 by Nestlé.
- Used to shrink and preserve food.
- Used by astronauts in space program.

GREEN REVOLUTION HELPS CURB STARVATION

By the 1940s, the population of Mexico was rising. Farmers were no longer able to grow enough food for everyone. American scientist Norman Borlaug made a new kind of wheat plant that produced more grain.

Borlaug noticed that larger seeds made plants with more grain to eat. The larger plants that grew from these seeds took in more sunlight. This helped them produce more grain. Borlaug selected plants with these traits and bred them together. Borlaug showed farmers in Mexico how to grow plants with the new seeds. They learned about fertilizers and better irrigation techniques. These methods helped them grow more grain per acre of land.

Improved irrigation systems were part of the Green Revolution.

By the 1960s, Mexican farmers were producing so much grain that they started to sell it to people in other countries. These techniques spread to countries in Asia, Africa, and India. They prevented many people from starving. This became known as the Green Revolution.

Over time, scientists learned more about farming technology. They found out that the fertilizers and pesticides used by Borlaug can be harmful to the environment.

New ways of farming are being developed that don't use as many unsafe chemicals.

1 billion
Approximate number of people the Green Revolution is credited with saving from starvation.

- Introduced by Norman Borlaug in the 1940s in Mexico.
- Spread to Asia, Africa, and India.
- New techniques let farmers grow more crops on less land.

Norman Borlaug won the Nobel Peace Prize in 1970 for his contributions to reducing world starvation.

FLASH-FREEZING SAVES FLAVOR AND NUTRITION

Food that freezes slowly forms large water crystals. These crystals break down the food's cells. But food that freezes quickly only forms small crystals. It keeps its texture and nutrients. Clarence Birdseye discovered this while fishing in the Arctic. It was so cold that when he pulled a fish from the water, it froze quickly. He noticed that if he ate the fish months later, it tasted like it had just been caught. Birdseye thought this method could be used on other foods.

In 1930, Birdseye patented a method for flash-freezing foods under pressure. He packaged the

The popularity of frozen foods led supermarkets to add large frozen food cases.

Flash-freezing prevents the formation of large ice crystals that affect taste.

frozen food in waxed cardboard. His company started selling frozen vegetables, fruits, seafood, and meats to the public. To make sure his products could reach the public, Birdseye also started marketing special frozen food cases to grocery stores. He leased refrigerated train cars to railroads. As more people started to have electric freezers in their homes, frozen foods surged in popularity. Frozen foods greatly increased the convenience and nutritional value of many foods.

168

Number of patents Birdseye held related to the flash-freezing method, covering the process, tools, and packaging.

- Patented by Clarence Birdseye in 1930.
- Alternative to canning that preserved taste and texture.
- Big advancement in preserving nutrients.

THINK ABOUT IT

Canning, flash-freezing, and freeze-drying are all methods of preserving foods. What are some of the advantages and disadvantages of each?

FLAVR SAVR TOMATO DESIGNED TO LAST LONGER

Farmers have been growing cross-pollinated crops for more than a century. They transferred pollen from one plant to another to breed plants with desired traits. As scientists learned more about how genes work, they started modifying plants in laboratories. They made plants that were easier to grow or resistant to insects. These are called genetically modified organisms (GMOs).

In 1994, a genetically modified tomato was sold in grocery stores for the first time. It was called the Flavr Savr tomato. Before the Flavr Savr, tomatoes were picked before they were ripe. This way they didn't spoil before reaching the grocery store. The Flavr Savr was designed to stay firm longer. This meant it could ripen fully on the vine for better flavor.

In the United States, 93 percent of soybean crops have been genetically modified.

GMO DEBATE

Major scientific groups have found GMO technology to be safe. The World Health Organization and the National Academy of Sciences have supported its use. But not everyone agrees. Critics think scientists should not tamper with genes. They argue that the practice could have unexpected results. It could hurt the environment or affect the food chain. Some countries have even banned GMOs.

After a few years, the company that made Flavr Savrs changed ownership. The tomatoes were taken off the market. But now many other crops are genetically modified. Some are resistant to insects. Others are designed to taste better, last longer, or contain more nutrients.

10

Percentage of the world's farmland that was being used to grow genetically modified crops by 2010.

- Flavr Savr tomatoes were introduced by the Calgene Company in 1994.
- First genetically modified food in grocery stores.
- Led to many other GMOs.

Genetically modified tomatoes have not been on the market since the 1990s. But other GMO crops are common.

FACT SHEET

- Many countries have a government agency in charge of safety issues related to food. In the United States, that agency is the Food and Drug Administration (FDA). The FDA inspects, tests, and approves food products. It sets safety standards for the industry. It can take legal action to stop the sale of harmful products.

- In the 1850s and 1860s, Gregor Mendel did experiments on pea plants. He discovered that genes determine plant characteristics. Mendel figured out how to breed different plants together by transferring pollen between them. He could control the color and shape of the flowers and peas. Scientists used his ideas to make better crops. They grew corn that insects wouldn't eat. They developed plants that grew faster and produced more food.

- Genetically modified crops can be designed to be naturally resistant to insects. Farmers using this technology have been able to reduce the use of insecticides. This lessens their costs and is better for the environment.

- Scientists are working on creating meats that don't come from live animals. They made a hamburger by growing cells from beef tissue in test tubes. Tasters tried the burger for the first time in London in 2013. The testers thought it tasted bland. But scientists still hope it could be an alternative to raising livestock in the future. Livestock use a lot of land, food, and water. Scientists think test-tube meat could help feed more people with less harm to the planet.

- NASA's Advanced Food Technology Project is researching better ways to prepare and package food for astronauts to take into space. They are working on a menu for an eventual trip to Mars. The goal is to design packaged foods with a shelf life of at least three years. The foods have to be nutritious. They also try to make foods that are as familiar as possible. This helps astronauts feel more at home while far away from Earth.

GLOSSARY

bacteria
Single-celled organisms that cause disease.

cross-pollinate
To transfer pollen from the flower of one plant to another.

drought
A long period of time with little or no rain.

fortified
Containing added nutrients.

gene
Part of the cells of a living thing that controls its traits.

hearth
The area in front of a fireplace.

irrigation
A system for watering crops.

microwave
A very short wave of electromagnetic energy.

modified
Changed in some ways but not others.

nutrients
Substances in foods or drinks that people need to live and grow.

organisms
Living things.

primitive
Simple and basic.

revolution
A sudden and extreme change in the way people do something.

supplement
Something added to a person's diet.

vapor
A substance in the form of a gas.

FOR MORE INFORMATION

Books

Higgins, Nadia. *Fun Food Inventions*. Minneapolis, MN: Lerner, 2014.

Latta, Sara L. *Microwave Man: Percy Spencer and His Sizzling Invention*. Berkeley Heights, NJ: Enslow, 2014.

Mason, Helen. *Agricultural Inventions: At the Top of the Field*. New York: Crabtree, 2013.

Mattern, Joanne. *Clarence Birdseye, Frozen Food Innovator*. Minneapolis, MN: Abdo, 2011.

Morris, Neil. *Food Technology*. North Mankato, MN: Capstone, 2012.

Websites

Penn State: Food Science for Kids of All Ages
foodscience.psu.edu/youth

US Department of Agriculture: USDA for Kids
www.usda.gov/wps/portal/usda/usdahome?navid=FOR_KIDS

US Food and Drug Administration: Food Safety and Nutrition Information for Kids and Teens
www.fda.gov/food/resourcesforyou/consumers/ucm2006971

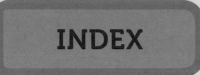
INDEX

Appert, Nicolas, 8

bacteria, 4, 9, 14–15
Birdseye, Clarence, 24–25
Borlaug, Norman, 22–23
breakfast cereal, 12–13

canning, 8–9
can openers, 9
cast-iron stoves, 10
cross-pollination, 26

Domestic Electric Refrigerator, 17
Durand, Peter, 9

edible food wrap, 15
electric refrigerators, 16–17

farming, 6–7, 22–23, 26
fertilizers, 22, 23
fire, 4–5, 10
flash-freezing, 24–25
Flavr Savr tomatoes, 26–27
food preservation, 8–9, 14–15, 20–21, 24–25
fortified foods, 18–19
freeze-drying, 20–21

gas stove, 10–11
genetically modified organisms, 26–27
goiters, 18–19
Granula, 12–13
Green Revolution, 22–23

iodized salt, 18–19
irrigation, 22

Jackson, James Caleb, 12

Kellogg, John, 13

microwave ovens, 11

Nestlé, 20

Pasteur, Louis, 14–15
pasteurization, 14–15

scurvy, 8
space food, 21

Wolf, Fred, 16

About the Author

Marne Ventura is a children's book author and a former elementary school teacher. She holds a master's degree in education with an emphasis in reading and language development from the University of California.

READ MORE FROM 12-STORY LIBRARY

Every 12-Story Library book is available in many formats, including Amazon Kindle and Apple iBooks. For more information, visit your device's store or 12StoryLibrary.com.